Applying the Standards:
Evidence-Based Reading
Grade 5

Credits
Content Editor: Christy Howard
Copy Editor: Elise Craver

Visit *carsondellosa.com* for correlations to Common Core, state, national, and Canadian provincial standards.

Carson-Dellosa Publishing, LLC
PO Box 35665
Greensboro, NC 27425 USA
carsondellosa.com

ISBN 978-1-4838-1463-6
02-215151151

Table of Contents

Title Page/Credits 1

Table of Contents 2

Introduction 2

Common Core Alignment Chart 3

Reading Comprehension Rubric 4

Literature Selections 5

Informational Text Selections 23

Answer Key 63

Introduction

The purpose of this book is to engage students in close reading while applying the standards. The Common Core reading and language strands are reflected in the interactive questions that follow each passage.

The lessons are intended to help students not only comprehend what they read superficially, but also to help them read complex texts closely and analytically. Students need to get involved deeply with what they are reading and use higher-order thinking skills to reflect on what they have read.

On the following activity pages, students will read a variety of literature and informational passages. These are brief but lend themselves to more complex thinking. Given the opportunity to study shorter texts, students can better practice the higher-level skills they need to closely read more demanding texts.

Each selection is followed by text-dependent questions. Students are prompted to pay attention to how a text is organized, to solve the question of why the author chose specific words, to look for deeper meaning, and to determine what the author is trying to say.

Use the included rubric to guide assessment of student responses and further plan any necessary remediation. The art of close reading is an invaluable skill that will help students succeed in their school years and beyond.

Common Core Alignment Chart

Use this chart to plan your instruction, practice, or remediation of a specific standard. To do this, first choose your targeted standard; then, find the pages listed on the chart that correlate to the standard.

Common Core State Standards*		Practice Pages
Reading Standards for Literature		
Key Ideas and Details	5.RL.1–5.RL.3	5–22
Craft and Structure	5.RL.4–5.RL.6	5–8, 10–18, 20–22
Integration of Knowledge and Ideas	5.RL.7, 5.RL.9	10, 12, 21, 22
Range of Reading and Level of Text Complexity	5.RL.10	Each reading passage can be adapted to exercise this standard.
Reading Standards for Informational Text		
Key Ideas and Details	5.RI.1–5.RI.3	23–61
Craft and Structure	5.RI.4–5.RI.6	23–27, 30–34, 37, 43–44, 46, 49–54, 57–60
Integration of Knowledge and Ideas	5.RI.7–5.RI.9	23, 26–28, 32, 34–38, 45–47, 49, 51, 52, 54–61
Range of Reading and Level of Text Complexity	5.RI.10	Each reading passage can be adapted to exercise this standard.
Reading Standards: Foundational Skills		
Fluency	5.RF.4	Each reading passage can be adapted to exercise this standard.
Language Standards		
Vocabulary Acquisition and Use	5.L.4–5.L.6	5–8, 10–14, 16, 17, 19, 20, 22–26, 32–34, 37, 44, 46, 50–54, 57–60

Reading Comprehension Rubric

Use this rubric as a guide to assess students' written work. It can also be offered to students to help them check their work or as a tool to show your scoring.

4	_____ Offers insightful reasoning and strong evidence of critical thinking
	_____ Makes valid, nontrivial inferences based on evidence in the text
	_____ Skillfully supports answers with relevant details from the text
	_____ Gives answers that indicate a complete understanding of the text
	_____ Gives answers that are easy to understand, clear, and concise
	_____ Uses conventions, spelling, and grammar correctly
3	_____ Offers sufficient reasoning and evidence of critical thinking
	_____ Makes inferences based on evidence in the text
	_____ Supports answers with details from the text
	_____ Gives answers that indicate a good understanding of the text
	_____ Gives answers that are easy to understand
	_____ Uses conventions, spelling, and grammar correctly most of the time
2	_____ Demonstrates some evidence of critical thinking
	_____ Makes incorrect inferences or does not base inferences on evidence in the text
	_____ Attempts to support answers with information from the text
	_____ Gives answers that indicate an incomplete understanding of the text
	_____ Gives answers that are understandable but lack focus
	_____ Gives answers containing several errors in conventions, spelling, and grammar
1	_____ Demonstrates limited or no evidence of critical thinking
	_____ Makes no inferences
	_____ Does not support answers with details from the text
	_____ Gives answers that indicate little to no understanding of the text
	_____ Gives answers that are difficult to understand
	_____ Gives answers with many errors in conventions, spelling, and grammar

Read. Then, answer the questions.

Night Noises

It is four o'clock in the morning. It is one of the few times when not-so-sleepyheads take the time to absorb the underlying sounds floating through dream-laden star scapes. It starts with a toss or a turn, a cough or a wheeze—some unidentified sound nudges me awake. Softly echoing at the base of my brain is the **incessant** chirp of a far-off cricket, strumming its children to sleep under a moist, brown blanket of leaves. The humming buzz of cicadas tickles my ears.

Aaaa . . . CHOO! It is enough to blow away any quiet-hour sounds. A cannon-shot nose blow continues my seven-hour viral war. The advertised soft tissue feels like sandpaper against my battle-torn nose. The lukewarm water left at my bedside soothes the screaming cells lining my aching throat.

A slight breeze tickles the curtains and plays with the maple leaves outside my window. It gently strokes my heated forehead and draws my burning eyes toward the soothing darkness. I drift between peaceful dreamland and the onslaught of a dripping nose and viral nasties tapping behind my tired eyes.

At sunup, a mourning dove whispers, asking if anyone else is awake. Another mourning dove sleepily answers, wondering who gave the wake-up call. I bury my head under my pillow, desperately searching for one last note from the stars.

1. In paragraph 3, the author says, "A slight breeze tickles the curtains." What type of figurative language is this? What does it mean?

   _____

   _____

2. At the end of the passage, what is the narrator wishing for? How do you know?

   _____

   _____

3. How does the narrator feel throughout the text?

   _____

   _____

❋ Reflect

Underline the examples of figurative language in the text. How might this story be different if the author did not use figurative language?

_____

_____

Name _____

Read. Then, answer the questions.

328

by Emily Dickinson

A Bird Came down the Walk—
He did not know I saw—
He bit an angle-worm in halves
And ate the fellow, raw,

And then he drank a Dew
From a convenient Grass,
And then hopped sidewise to the Wall
To let a Beetle pass—

He glanced with rapid eyes
That hurried all abroad—
They looked like frightened Beads, I thought—
He stirred his Velvet Head.

Like one in danger, **Cautious**,
I offered him a Crumb,
And he unrolled his feathers
And rowed him softer home—

Than Oars divide the Ocean,
Too silver for a seam—
Or Butterflies, off Banks of Noon,
Leap, splashless as they swim.

1. What does *cautious* mean? Why do you think the narrator was cautious when she offered the bird a crumb?

_____

_____

2. How does the author organize each stanza of the poem? How do the stanzas fit together to tell a story?

_____

_____

3. Summarize the poem in your own words.

_____

_____

_____

Reflect

How might this poem, especially stanza 4, be different if the narrator was the bird?

_____

_____

_____

_____

 © Carson-Dellosa · CD-104834 · Applying the Standards: Evidence-Based Reading

Name _____

Read. Then, answer the questions on page 8.

The White Heron
by Sarah Orne Jewett (adapted)

Half a mile from Shelby's home, at the edge of the woods, stood a great pine tree. The tree was a landmark that could be seen from many miles away. Shelby had always believed that anyone who climbed to the top of the tree would be able to see the ocean and maybe all of the world. The little girl had often laid her hand on the tree's great trunk and looked up at the dark boughs. She wondered if, by climbing the tree, she could discover where the white heron flew and find its hidden nest. She decided that she would try.

The windows of the little house were open all night, and the whip-poor-wills sang outside Shelby's room. Everyone else was asleep, but Shelby's plan kept her awake. The short summer night seemed as long as the winter darkness. At last, she crept out of the house and followed the path through the woods. A sleepy bird chirped nearby.

Finally, she came to the huge tree asleep in the moonlight. Small and hopeful, Shelby bravely climbed. Her bare feet and fingers pinched and held like bird claws to the tree. The tree seemed to reach farther and farther upward as she climbed, but Shelby felt her way easily.

Shelby's face was like a pale star as she stood in the treetop. Yes, there was the sea, glinting with the golden dazzle of the sunrise. Toward the east flew two hawks. Their gray feathers were as soft as moths; they seemed only a little way from the tree. Westward, the woodlands and farms reached for miles into the distance, and here and there were church steeples and white villages. Truly, it was a huge and awesome world.

The birds sang louder, and at last, the sun came up bewilderingly bright. Shelby could see the white sails of ships at sea. The clouds that had been purple, rose, and yellow began to fade. Shelby began to look for the white heron's nest from her perch in the magnificent tree.

Shelby looked toward the green marsh. There, she saw a white spot, like a single floating feather, rise and drift toward the pine tree with a sweep of wings, an outstretched, slender neck, and a crested head. Shelby crouched silently in the tree, watching the heron. It perched on a nearby branch. It gave a cry to its mate on the nest and shook its feathers to welcome the new day.

Shelby gave a sigh. She knew the bird's secret now, the wild, light, slender bird that floats and wavers and goes back like an arrow to his home in the great green world.

Name _____

Read the story on page 7. Then, answer the questions.

1. What inferences can you make about Shelby? Use evidence from the text to support your inferences.

_____

_____

_____

2. What does the narrator mean when he says, "the short summer night seemed as long as the winter darkness"?

_____

_____

3. In the third paragraph the narrator says, "Her bare feet and fingers pinched and held like bird claws to the tree." What kind of figurative language is this? Why do you think the author makes this comparison?

_____

_____

_____

4. What was the secret Shelby discovered at the end of the story?

_____

_____

_____

Reflect

How does Shelby feel about nature? What does the author do throughout the story to let you know this? Cite evidence from the text to support your answer.

_____

_____

_____

_____

_____

_____

_____

 © Carson-Dellosa · CD-104834 · Applying the Standards: Evidence-Based Reading

Name _____

Read. Then, answer the questions.

New Year's Day

Early in the morning on January 1, Jason is wide awake. He gets up and takes his dog outside for a walk. When he comes in, he gets a glass of juice and watches television. Soon, his parents get up, and his dad starts making a special breakfast of waffles, eggs, and fresh fruit. Jason knows that taking down the holiday decorations is the job of the day, so he gathers boxes from the garage and brings them into the house.

After breakfast, the whole family takes down decorations. Jason's dad reminds Jason and his mom that the college football bowl games will begin at one o'clock in the afternoon. Jason and his mom carefully take down all of the decorations in the family room. They hand them to Jason's father, who wraps each one in tissue paper and places it in a box for next year. Jason helps his father wrap the decorations while his mom travels from room to room collecting the rest of the holiday decorations.

Soon, everything is packed, and the boxes are stored for next year. The television displays spectacular floats and spirited performers as the parade spirals through the routes of adoring bystanders. Jason's mom prepares a traditional lunch of hot dogs, chips, and dip. His mom says that it is good luck to eat cabbage on New Year's Day, so they eat sauerkraut with their hot dogs. Jason doesn't like cabbage, but he takes some anyway. They get comfortable in front of the television to watch the football games.

The day is one big vacation, and Jason loves it. His family is together, there is plenty of food, and the college football games are fun to watch. The new year cannot be bad if it starts off like this!

1. Summarize the story in your own words.

   _____

   _____

2. What can you infer about Jason's father? Why?

   _____

   _____

3. Why does Jason like New Year's Day so much? How do you know?

   _____

   _____

☀ Reflect

How does the author organize the story? How does it help you understand the story?

_____

_____

Name _____

Read. Then, answer the questions.

Soccer Champions

Alicia is on the championship soccer team, the Mongooses. Her team had five wins, two ties, and one loss in the regular season. Alicia was the team's primary goalie. When not playing goalie, she alternated between defense and offense. Alicia was the **exclusive** goalie during play-offs. See the play-off bracket below.

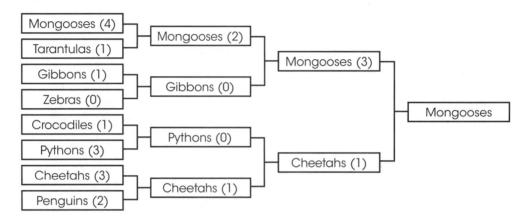

1. How many teams were in the play-offs?

_____

2. Based on the text, how many games did Alicia play in regular season?

_____

3. What does *exclusive* mean? How do you know?

_____

_____

4. What can you infer about Alicia? Use evidence from the text to support your answer.

_____

_____

☀ Reflect

Who won first and second place in the championship? How does the chart of Alicia's games help you to answer this question?

_____

_____

_____

Name _____

Read. Then, answer the questions.

Winter Is a White Owl

by Alisha Golden

The owl's eyes shine darkly,
As the quiet moon at midnight.
So chillingly cold,
So dark and black.
The snow falls gently,
Like the downy feathers
Of the night watcher.
He floats from tree to limb,
Ever watchful,
In the frosty winter night.
The moon casts her pale light
On the soft snow.
Nature is in silent **slumber**,
Deeply buried
Under a blanket of white crystals.
The owl is alone,
Except for the moon.
All is still.

1. What does *slumber* mean?

_____

2. What does the narrator compare the falling snow to? What type of figurative
language is this?

_____

_____

3. What is the mood of this poem? How do you know?

_____

_____

Reflect

How does the author's word choice help you to see images in your mind as you read
the poem? Why do you think the author chose these words?

_____

_____

_____

Name _____

Read the poems on pages 11 and 12. Then, answer the questions.

Winter Sunrise

By J. P. Wallaker

Rose fingernails push back
star-sparkled blanket.
Warm toes slide out,
feel cold morning.
Pink pajama-clad body sits on side of bed,
shivering,
standing,
stretching.
Sparkle . . .
A snow day.

1. What does the author compare the sunrise to?

   _____

2. Underline an example of alliteration in the poem. How are these words related?

   _____

   _____

3. What does the "star-sparkled blanket" represent in this poem?

   _____

4. Compare and contrast "Winter Sunrise" to "Winter is a White Owl."

   _____

   _____

   _____

Reflect

What words does the author use to create imagery in the poem? What do these words help you visualize?

_____

_____

_____

_____

_____

Name _____

Read. Then, answer the questions on page 14.

Amy's Swim Meet

When she got to the pool, Amy hardly recognized the **natatorium** as the same place where she practiced every week. The starting blocks were crowded with judges and timers. Banners for the different teams hung from the wall opposite the bleachers. And, the bleachers were actually filled with people: parents, grandparents, brothers, sisters, and a lot of swimmers from different teams. The noise of all of those people and the announcer calling warm-up pool assignments was really loud. Amy saw her friend Mia and went to find out where the rest of the team was.

"Look!" Mia exclaimed when she saw Amy. "We're in the same heat for backstroke and breaststroke."

Amy grinned at her friend. "Cool," she said. "Can I borrow your program to see when all of my events are?"

Amy looked at the program. She was swimming the 50-meter backstroke, the 50-meter breaststroke, the 100-meter freestyle, and both of the medley and freestyle relays. According to the program, she would have only a few minutes between the backstroke and breaststroke events. It looked like she would have time to eat lunch between her breaststroke and freestyle events, but she would have to swim the relays right after her freestyle event. She put down her stuff and went to the warm-up pool to swim some laps with Mia.

Soon after they got out of the warm-up pool, it was time for their backstroke event. They stepped onto the blocks and waited for the starter to tell them to jump into the water and take their marks. Mia started faster than Amy, but Amy caught her at the turn and beat her by half of a length. Later, in the breaststroke event, Amy sucked in some water and stopped to cough before rallying to finish third behind Mia and another teammate.

After lunch, Amy swam a record for her age group in the 100-meter freestyle. She and Mia swam with two other girls from their team and won both relays. By the end of the day, Amy was exhausted, but she had earned four first-place finishes and one third-place finish. It had been her best performance at a swim meet, and she was proud of her effort.

Name _____

Read the story on page 13. Then, answer the questions.

1. What can you infer about Amy and Mia? How are they alike? How are they different? Use evidence from the text to support your answer.

_____

_____

_____

2. How does Amy feel about the differences she notices in paragraph 1?

_____

_____

3. What did the program reveal to Amy?

_____

_____

4. What is a *natatorium*? How do you know?

_____

_____

Reflect

How might the story be different if it were told from Mia's point of view?

_____

_____

_____

_____

_____

_____

_____

_____

_____

_____

Read. Then, answer the questions.

Snow

The landscape was a sparkling, blinding whiteness. The rare hours of sunshine managed to locate each and every snowflake on the surface of the snow, using it to magnify and reflect its brightness. Candice and Sasha were outside with a crystal chart, trying to identify snowflake types. They had already identified stellar dendrites, hexagonal plates, needle crystals, and powder snow this winter. They were hoping to mark off the spatial dendrites or column crystals today. Sasha was holding a smattering of flakes on a piece of black fabric. Candice had taken off one mitten and put it in her pocket and held the magnifying glass with her bare hand. The girls heard a noise and looked up. The snow shimmer temporarily blinded them, preventing them from seeing the large white shape leaping across the yard. WHAM! The dog barreled into both girls. Candice fell backwards into a snowbank and came up sputtering. "Down, Tiny!" she demanded. "Get off me!" Her hand was wet, red, and icy. The magnifying glass was nowhere to be seen. Sasha had fallen facedown. Tiny's hind legs were in the middle of her back, preventing Sasha from getting to her feet. Tiny finally leaped off Sasha to grab the black square of fabric. Tug-of-war was his favorite game after "knock down."

1. What effect did the sun have on the snow?

   _____

   _____

2. What was the effect of Tiny barreling into Candice? Use evidence from the text to support your answer.

   _____

   _____

3. How does Tiny feel about the girls? How do you know?

   _____

   _____

☀ Reflect

How would Tiny have described the game of "knock down"? Think about how it would be different from the girls' point of view.

_____

_____

_____

_____

Read. Then, answer the questions.

Housefly

Swak! The flyswatter hit the table for yet another near miss. A fly buzzed **tauntingly** just above Jeff's head. It relaxed and landed on the edge of the window. Smik! Jan tallied her tenth kill in a row. "Absolutely no way!" yelled Jeff. "There is no way you can get those flies every time!"

"Good thing for you I can," said Jan. "You left the sliding door open and let all those flies come right into the house. You know Mom will have a fit if they're still in here at dinnertime." Smack! Jan landed another one as if to prove her point.

Swak! Swak! Swak! Jeff missed three more, the sweat running down his face as much from effort as from the heat. "Okay, I give. How do you do it? Last week you couldn't hit a fly if it was the size of a bird. This week you can't miss."

"It's knowledge, you know," Jan said. "I checked out a book from the library and found out something interesting about these flies—they take off backwards."

"What!?"

"Backwards. When a fly takes off, it goes backwards, then shoots off forwards. If you aim right behind their little behinds, you get them every time."

Jeff grinned as he eyed his latest prey.

1. What does *tauntingly* mean? How do you know?

_____

_____

2. Compare and contrast Jan and Jeff.

_____

_____

3. Why is Jeff surprised Jan is hitting all of the flies? Use evidence from the text to support your answers.

_____

_____

☀ Reflect

Why does the author use the words "swak," "smik," and "smack"?

_____

_____

_____

Read. Then, answer the questions.

An Ant's Life

Harry lugged the sandwich crumb through one tunnel after another. It was a relief to be out of the blazing sunlight. His downward journey was made in the company of thousands of his fellow six-footed colonists. He was tired—weary, but still going. He knew the need for food was all-important. Still, that story haunted him. The one about the grasshopper and the ant. Yes, they did have food to eat and a safe, warm home, but wasn't fun necessary, too? Harry had talked to Granny about it. "You can't fill your belly with fun or stay alive on daydreams," had been her reply. "Be happy with your existence." Harry walked slowly from the storage area, still depressed and thoughtful. A half hour wouldn't hurt, would it? He could grab extra crumbs during the rest of the day. He would still do his part. Besides, wouldn't he be more productive after having a little rest or a bit of fun? He looked towards the sunlit opening of the ant hill. A smile spread slowly across his face. There were plenty of **detours** available between the ant hill and that picnic.

1. Summarize Harry's problem.

_____

_____

2. How are Granny and Harry different? Use evidence from the text to support your answer.

_____

_____

3. What are *detours*? How do you know?

_____

_____

🔆 Reflect

Why do you think the author told the story from Harry's point of view? How might the story be different if it were told from Granny's point of view?

_____

_____

_____

_____

Read. Then, answer the questions.

Chef Wendy's Special Ingredient

Wendy wanted to surprise her mom and her mom's boyfriend, Tony, with a spaghetti dinner. She knew that Tony always came over on Friday nights.

Wendy planned ahead. On Wednesday, she asked her mom to get ground beef, an onion, tomato sauce, spaghetti noodles, and ingredients for salad. Her mom gave her an odd look, but she did not say anything. She figured that her mother had caught on, but because she did not say anything, Wendy knew that she would keep the secret.

On Friday, as soon as she got home from school, Wendy started making dinner. Her babysitter chopped the onion and helped Wendy brown the ground beef and onion in a skillet. Wendy remembered that she had not eaten her snack from lunch—a chocolate candy bar. She got it out of her book bag, opened it, and took a bite. It was so good! Then, with her candy bar in her hand, she went to the counter to mix the spaghetti sauce. Somehow, as Wendy was pouring the tomato sauce over the ground beef, she accidentally dropped the rest of the candy bar into the sauce!

Just then, Wendy's mom and Tony came home and followed the smell into the kitchen.

"Mmm, spaghetti," Tony said, "my favorite!" Wendy just smiled and stirred the sauce.

Later, when they sat down to eat, Wendy's mother and Tony both bragged about the spaghetti. Tony even had a second helping! Wendy secretly thought that the sauce tasted funny, but everyone else said that it was the best spaghetti they had ever had. From then on, Wendy was the head spaghetti chef in the house!

1. How does Wendy feel about Tony? How do you know this?

_____

2. What does Wendy do to prepare for Friday night?

_____

3. What are two character traits that describe Wendy? Use evidence from the text to support your answer.

_____

_____

☀ Reflect

How might the story be different if it were told from Wendy's mom's point of view? What might be revealed to the reader?

_____

_____

Name _____

Read. Then, answer the questions.

From Tomboy to Ballerina

When I was young, I never wanted to be a dancer. I always wanted to play the same sports as my brother, like soccer, hockey, and basketball. In my mind, ballet was not really a sport.

I tried playing a lot of sports and did OK, but I was never very good at any of them except soccer. Even though I practiced a lot and tried my best, there was always one problem: I was small. I was spunky, but I always got pushed around by bigger players. So, I decided to try dancing.

In the beginning, I was clumsy and had no sense of balance. I did not have a graceful bone in my body. For the first few months, my weekly lessons were disasters, but I did not quit. If I could choose one word to describe my attitude, it would be **stubborn**. I refused to give up. Because of my dedication, hard work, and resolve, I got better and better until I found myself dancing in a studio almost daily.

I love to dance! Sometimes, it is just plain hard, and other days, I really enjoy myself. Our teacher yells out corrections and choreographed steps to the class as we dance. The violinist plays beautifully. The notes carry me into the sky. I feel as if I am flying on the music. Soaring, I cannot feel the ground beneath me. My tutu rustles softly as my shoes patter on the floor with every step. My legs and arms move and extend in harmony with the music. Every part of my body moves as gracefully as a summer breeze. I feel more alive than ever. Fatigue is miles away. I am going to be a ballerina. I can never give up this passion, even though the pain in my toes stings and screams for me to stop. I love to dance!

1. Why didn't the narrator feel successful in soccer? How do you know?

_____

2. What evidence does the narrator use to support the idea that she is stubborn?

_____

_____

3. How does the narrator change from the beginning of the story to the end?

_____

_____

✺ Reflect

Underline the figurative language in the last paragraph. How does the use of figurative language affect the story?

_____

_____

Name _____

Read. Then, answer the questions.

Eldorado
by Edgar Allan Poe

Gaily bedight,
A **gallant** knight,
In sunshine and in shadow,
    Had journeyed long,
    Singing a song,
In search of Eldorado.

But he grew old—
This knight so bold—
And o'er his heart a shadow
    Fell as he found
    No spot of ground
That looked like Eldorado.

And, as his strength
    Failed him at length,
He met a pilgrim shadow—
    "Shadow," said he,
    "Where can it be—
This land of Eldorado?"

"Over the Mountains
    Of the Moon,
Down the Valley of the Shadow,
    Ride, boldly ride,"
    The shade replied,—
"If you seek for Eldorado!"

1. What does *gallant* mean? How do you know?

_____

_____

2. What is the mood of this poem? What words help to reveal the mood?

_____

_____

3. Does the knight find Eldorado? How do you know?

_____

_____

Reflect

How do the stanzas show how the knight changes throughout the poem?

_____

_____

_____

_____

_____

Name _____

Read. Then, answer the questions.

Jar of Life

Have you ever heard of the "jar of life"? You only get to fill it once. Rocks are the most important things in life, like family and health. They are the things you cannot bear to live without. Pebbles are the next order of priorities: school, jobs, friends, and important items. Sand is the fun and the "stuff."

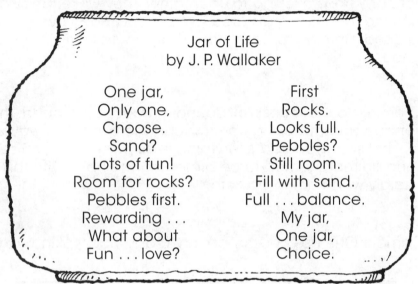

Jar of Life
by J. P. Wallaker

One jar,   First
Only one,   Rocks.
Choose.   Looks full.
Sand?   Pebbles?
Lots of fun!   Still room.
Room for rocks?   Fill with sand.
Pebbles first.   Full . . . balance.
Rewarding . . .   My jar,
What about   One jar,
Fun . . . love?   Choice.

1. What is the theme of this poem?

_____

2. From the narrator's point of view, what happens if you only fill the jar with sand, or the "fun stuff"?

_____

3. How does the speaker show pride and ownership of his jar?

_____

_____

✷ Reflect

How does the image of the poem inside the jar add meaning to the poem?

_____

_____

_____

_____

Name _____

Read. Then, answer the questions.

Camping on Frog Pond

Read two campers' descriptions of waking up on Frog Pond. Then answer the questions.

Camper One

   We woke this morning to waves lapping the shore, a breeze rustling the leaves, and the sounds of sweet baby frogs cricking to each other. They woke the swans and ducks who sang good morning to the animals around the pond. Soon every insect, bird, and animal was calling good morning to each other. How could I stay in bed? I needed to greet the morning, too.

Camper Two

   We woke this morning to the **incessant** sound of frogs in the pond. Their shrill alarm triggered off-key honking and quacking from around the pond. The waves slapped the shore while the wind sandpapered everything in its path. Within 60 seconds, every insect, bird, and animal seemed to be protesting the hour. With this **cacophony** continuing, it was hardly worth going back to sleep.

1. How does Camper One use personification to describe waking up on Frog Pond?

_____

2. What does *incessant* mean? How do you know?

_____

_____

3. How do the word choices made by Camper Two, like *incessant* and *cacophony*, explain that camper's point of view?

_____

_____

☀ Reflect

Compare and contrast the two stories from the campers. How are the speakers' perspectives similar? How are they different?

_____

_____

_____

_____

Name _____

Read. Then, answer the questions.

The Unicorn and the Rhinoceros

The unicorn is an animal described in ancient Greek and Indian myths. The unicorn was said to look like a horse with a horn protruding from the front of its head.

The horn was described as being straight with a spiral twist. It was also described as being white at the base, black in the middle, and red at the tip. A colorful animal, the unicorn was said to have a white body, a red head, and blue eyes. According to one source, its hind legs were like an antelope's and its tail was like a lion's.

The truth is that no one has ever seen a unicorn because unicorns do not exist. However, this has not kept people from believing that they have seen unicorns.

In the Dark Ages or the very early Middle Ages, some of the earliest European explorers ventured east to Asia. Much of Asia was different from Europe. The land and people looked different, and there were different types of plants. Some of the animals there were different from any creatures that the European explorers had ever seen.

These European explorers probably saw a rhinoceros among the wonders of Asia. When they returned to Europe, they told of the beautiful silk fabrics, the **exotic** teas and spices, and the amazing animals they saw. They probably told stories of a creature that was bigger than a horse with a horn growing out of the front of its head. This creature could also run as fast as a horse for a short period of time. The people hearing these stories had never seen a rhinoceros. The only thing that they could imagine was a large horse with a horn on its head, or the unicorn picture that we know today.

1. Why did some early explorers believe they had seen unicorns? Underline evidence in the text that supports your answer.

   _____

2. The narrator says the land in Asia was different from the land in Europe. How does the author support this point?

   _____

   _____

3. What does *exotic* mean?

   _____

☀ Reflect

How does the comparison of the rhinocerous, horse, and unicorn help the author make the point about where the myth came from?

_____

_____

_____

Name _____

Read. Then, answer the questions on page 25.

John Colter: Western Explorer

John Colter died at a young age, but before he did, he saw and explored more of the American wilderness than nearly any European explorer of his time. He was one of the first settlers to cross North America and see the Pacific Ocean. He traveled through the territories of some hostile American Indians. He saw amazing natural wonders. The stories that he told about his adventures were so fantastic that people did not always believe him.

Colter was born around 1774 in Virginia. In 1804, he set off into the unknown wilderness of the American West. He traveled with a group called the Corps of Discovery. The Corps included 31 other men, a teenage girl named Sacagawea, and her baby. Their goal was to find a waterway that connected the Missouri River and the Pacific Ocean. Two army captains named Lewis and Clark led the group. The corps members suffered hardship, hunger, sickness, and fatigue, but the journey made them famous.

After nearly two years in the wilderness, the Corps of Discovery was headed back to St. Louis, Missouri. As they neared a Mandan village in what is now North Dakota, they met a company of fur trappers coming up the Missouri River. The company was eager to gain information about the wilderness, so Colter decided to stay and be their guide.

On one of his trips to trap animals for furs, Colter came across the strangest landscape that he had ever seen. Water boiled from the earth and shot 70 feet (21.33 m) into the air. Thick mud bubbled from stinking pools and filled the air with a foul stench. All kinds of wild animals roamed freely through this land of **peculiar** beauty.

Colter had wandered into an area that the local American Indians called the Land of Fire. Today, we call the area Yellowstone National Park. Some people who heard his amazing stories and his descriptions of boiling pools and steam coming from the earth at Yellowstone thought that Colter had made them up.

John Colter lived a life of adventure. But, how did he die? Did he fall with an arrow in his chest? Did he die in the harsh elements of the wild? No one knows for sure, but many historians believe that his death was neither violent nor heroic. According to some accounts, Colter was living on a Missouri farm in 1813 when he died in his bed of a disease called jaundice.

Read the passage on page 24. Then, answer the questions.

1. What are two main ideas of this text? Write two supporting details for each main idea.

   Main Idea: _____

      Detail: _____

      Detail: _____

   Main Idea: _____

      Detail: _____

      Detail: _____

2. What can you infer about John Colter? Use evidence from the text to support your answer.

   _____

   _____

   _____

3. What does *peculiar* mean? How do you know? Use *peculiar* in a sentence related to what you learned about John Colter.

   _____

   _____

   _____

☀ Reflect

The author states that the American Indians used to call Yellowstone Park the Land of Fire. Based on the description, why do you think it was called the Land of Fire?

_____

_____

_____

_____

_____

_____

Name _____

Read. Then, answer the questions on page 27.

John Colter's Escape

John Colter was an explorer who traveled with Lewis and Clark across North America. He trapped animals for furs, explored new country, and survived in a harsh wilderness. He became a legend when he escaped from a tribe of American Indians who chased him for five miles across cactus-covered prairies and sharp volcanic rock.

It happened in Wyoming in 1809. Members of the Blackfoot tribe suddenly surrounded John Colter and his traveling companion, John Potts. The American Indians shot Potts and captured Colter. They took Colter's clothes and shoes, and they held a council to decide his fate. Colter could understand some of their language, and he heard them discussing how to kill him. The chief asked him, "Can you run fast?"

"No," Colter said. However, years of living in the wilderness had made him physically fit and vigorous. He was scared for his life, and the will to live burned within him. The chief told Colter to start walking away from the camp. After he had walked a few hundred yards, someone yelled. All of the braves in the camp sprinted after him.

The Yellowstone River was five miles away. Colter knew that if he could get to the river, he might have a chance of escaping the tribe. The ground was rough and covered with sharp rocks and prickly pear cacti. The braves wore thick moccasins. Colter raced for his life on bare feet. The soles of his feet were soon covered with cactus needles. His lungs felt ready to explode in the thin, mountain air. Several braves were gaining on him. He could have given up, but his will to live roared like a great fire within him. He pushed himself to run faster.

He called upon every bit of strength and energy he had in his body. After a couple of miles, his nose started to bleed **profusely**. At last, he reached the river and dove in. The icy water washed away the blood and soothed his torn feet. He hid under a logjam as the braves searched for him on both sides of the river. The tired trapper stayed in the river until dark. Then, he crawled out to finish his escape. He climbed a mountain in the dark and finally stumbled into a trading post a few weeks later.

His arrival at the trading post led to one of the most important discoveries that he ever made. It was a discovery about himself. Although John Colter marched with the Corps of Discovery, blazed trails, explored a vast wilderness, and discovered fabulous geysers, his greatest discovery was learning how strong the will to live could be.

Name _____

Read the passages on pages 24 and 26. Then, answer the questions.

1. What are two character traits that describe John Colter? Use evidence from the texts to support your answer.

_____

_____

_____

2. Explain the relationship between John Colter and the American Indians. How did the American Indians feel about Colter? How did he feel about them?

_____

_____

_____

3. What does *profusely* mean? How do you know? Use *profusely* in a sentence related to what you learned about John Colter.

_____

_____

_____

☀ Reflect

Compare and contrast the two stories, "John Colter: Western Explorer" and "John Colter's Escape." What new information do you learn about John Colter in "John Colter's Escape"?

_____

_____

_____

_____

_____

_____

_____

Name _____

Read. Then, answer the questions on page 29.

A Pioneer of Flight

Amelia Earhart saw an airplane for the first time at a state fair when she was 10 years old.

"It was a thing of rusty wire and wood and looked not at all interesting," she said. Not until a decade later, while attending a stunt-flying exhibition, did she really become interested in flying.

She rode in an airplane for the first time in 1920. As a social worker, Earhart had never had any experience with planes. Determined to learn how to fly, she took her first lesson on January 3, 1921. In just six months, she saved enough money to buy her own plane. It was a bright yellow Kinner Airster nicknamed "Canary." She set her first record in it by becoming the first woman to fly to an altitude of 14,000 feet.

Earhart flew constantly. Her hard work paid off in April 1928 when a book publisher and publicist named George P. Putnam asked her if she would fly across the Atlantic Ocean. Her answer was "Yes!" She was only a passenger on the historic flight between Newfoundland and Wales, but she returned to the United States as a celebrity.

From that point on, Earhart's life centered around flying. She became popular as she won competitions and awards. Though she had been shy before, people thought that she was witty, charming, and intelligent. Her fans loved the fact that she looked so much like Charles Lindbergh, another great aviator of the time. Many people called her "Lady Lindy."

Earhart married George Putnam on February 7, 1931. Together, they planned her solo trek across the Atlantic Ocean, which began on May 20, 1932. When she returned home, the media surrounded her as President Herbert Hoover awarded her a gold medal from the National Geographic Society. More medals followed. But, she did not stop there. On January 11, 1935, she became the first person to fly solo from Honolulu, Hawaii, to Oakland, California.

As her 40th birthday drew close, Earhart set a new goal. She wanted to be the first woman to fly around the world. Despite a failed first attempt in March 1937 and a damaged plane, a determined Earhart departed from Miami, Florida, on June 1, 1937. Navigator Fred Noonan accompanied her.

They had completed all but 7,000 miles (11,265 km) of the 29,000 mile (46,671 km) journey when they disappeared over the Pacific Ocean. Earhart was heading for a small island, but she missed the island because of cloudy conditions. Her plane never landed. A rescue attempt began immediately. It soon became the most extensive search for a single plane ever made by the US Navy. They never found Earhart or her plane, but she lives on as a legend in aviation history.

Name _____

Read the passage on page 28. Then, answer the questions.

1. What made Amelia Earhart change her opinion about airplanes?

_____

_____

_____

2. What is one inference you can make about Amelia Earhart? Use evidence from the text to support your inference.

_____

_____

_____

3. The passage states that Earhart's life centered on flying. What evidence does the author give to support this statement?

_____

_____

_____

☀ Reflect

The author ends by saying Amelia Earhart lives on as a legend. Why do you think the author calls her a legend? Use evidence from the text to support your answer.

_____

_____

_____

_____

_____

_____

_____

_____

Name _____

Read. Then, answer the questions on page 31.

Backyard Discoveries

My Cherry Tree House
by Kristen Diebele

I yawned, sat up, and wiped the sleep from my eyes. I did not want to leave the warmth of my comfortable bed. I got up reluctantly, sighed, and stretched. Then, I was ready to start my day. My goal that morning was to go to the large cherry tree in the center of my yard. My grandpa had built a tree house for me there, and it was my special place away from the world.

I climbed the heavy, wooden ladder and steadied myself. Then, I sat on the tree house's rough, wooden floor. I gazed at the ripe cherries, swollen with juice, ready to burst like fat little balloons. Usually, the cherries were gone because the blue jays had eaten them, but there were many cherries left. The birds must have slept in that day.

The branches drooped with cherries, and I plucked one from a branch. I swung the cherry back and forth like the pendulum of a clock. My tongue felt around my mouth for a tooth that was chipped from biting into a cherry last summer. I leaned over and squeezed the cherry until the pit fell to the ground. Then, I lay back to look at the morning.

That was four years ago. Now, I am 13 years old. The tree house grew old and rotten; it fell to the ground. My grandfather, who built the tree house, passed away. Things have changed, and so have I. Although my tree house does not exist anymore, I have not lost my special place. My tree house and my grandpa are in a special place in my mind. It is someplace I can go no matter where I am in the world.

White Sands National Monument
by Matt Kendell

The dunes at White Sands National Monument in New Mexico look like snow-covered hills with plants sticking out. People can climb up and sled down many of the dunes. If you look closely, the sand looks like salt. It is made from a mineral called gypsum. Usually, gypsum is mixed with rainwater and washed to sea. It is rarely found in desert sand.

There are paths in parts of the dunes that have signs telling about the plants and animals that live there. A lot of plants live in the dunes. One plant, called the yucca, holds the sand around it in place with its roots. The wind blows away the sand, but some sand stays stuck in the roots and it looks like a stump.

Many animals live among the dunes. Sometimes, you can see a lizard hiding under a bush or running away from people. There are also coyotes, rabbits, and foxes there. Most of them hide in burrows during the day to keep from overheating. Many animals have adopted a white color for camouflage. It is hard for plants and animals to live in the dunes because their homes in the sand are often moved by the wind. In fact, at first glance, you might not think that anything lives there at all. But, if you look closely, you might be surprised by what you see.

Name _____

Read the passages on page 30. Then, answer the questions.

1. In the essay, "My Cherry Tree House," how does the author feel about the tree house? How do you know?

_____

_____

_____

2. Describe the narrator of "My Cherry Tree House." How does the narrator's point of view influence the description of this special place?

_____

_____

_____

3. In "White Sands National Monument," what is special about the yucca plant? Use evidence from the text to support your answer.

_____

_____

_____

4. What are the two main ideas in "White Sands National Monument"? Give one supporting detail for each main idea.

Main Idea: _____

Detail: _____

Main Idea: _____

Detail: _____

Reflect

Compare and contrast "My Cherry Tree House" and "White Sands National Monument."

_____

_____

_____

_____

Name _____

Read. Then, answer the questions on page 33.

The Florida Keys

111 Sunset Cove
Key West, FL 33040

March 5, 2008

Dear Mom,

I am having a great time on my vacation through the Florida Keys! It is hard to believe that so much beauty is just a few hours away from the mainland of Florida. I have learned many interesting things on my trip that I want to share with you.

First, did you know that these islands are home to many endangered species? The key deer, the manatee, and the green sea turtle all make their homes in the Florida Keys. The people who live in this part of Florida are very protective of the local wildlife. For example, in Big Pine Key, home of the key deer, there are very strict laws against speeding on the highway. The miniature key deer are prone to running onto the road, just like their larger cousins. Fines are high for speeding in Big Pine Key.

Manatees often live in the warm waters of the boat canals that lead to the ocean. There are restrictions put on boaters to encourage them to be watchful of these gentle giants. People who live along the canals are discouraged from feeding these seafaring mammals because they may become too dependent on human help for survival. Residents of the Florida Keys seem to genuinely care about the environment.

Another interesting aspect of the Florida Keys is the amazing Seven Mile Bridge that stretches between the city of Marathon and the Lower Keys. The bridge really is seven miles (11.26 km) long! The remains of the old Seven Mile Bridge stand right next to the new Seven Mile Bridge. Many people **amble** along the old structure or fish from its sides. The Seven Mile Bridge is the longest segmented bridge in the world. The view from this bridge as we drove across it was spectacular. On one side, we saw the beautiful turquoise waters of the Gulf of Mexico. On the other, we saw the majestic Atlantic Ocean.

Key West is a very popular tourist spot. I learned that in this city, I can visit the home of Ernest Hemingway, tour an old naval base, and stand on the spot that is exactly 90 miles from the island nation of Cuba! I have enjoyed walking the historic streets, admiring the beautiful architecture, and eating all of the delicious food. Some people say that the sunsets in Key West are the best in Florida. We went to the top of a hotel to watch one, and it was fantastic!

I am sure that you can tell that I am enjoying my vacation in the Florida Keys. I think that it may be the best vacation spot in the United States. I will see you soon!

Love,

Anne

Name _____

Read the letter on page 32. Then, answer the questions.

1. What are two main ideas of this text? Write two supporting details for each main idea.

   Main Idea: _____

       Detail: _____

       Detail: _____

   Main Idea: _____

       Detail: _____

       Detail: _____

2. The author says people are protective of the wildlife and care of the environment. What evidence supports this statement?

   _____

   _____

   _____

3. What does *amble* mean? How do you know? Write a synonym for *amble*.

   _____

   _____

4. What can you infer about Anne? Use evidence from the text to support your inference.

   _____

   _____

   _____

☀ Reflect

At the end of the passage, Anne tells her mother she thinks this may be the best vacation spot in the United States. How does she support this statement throughout the letter?

_____

_____

_____

_____

Read. Then, answer the questions.

The Supreme Court

Originally, the number of justices who sat on the United States Supreme Court varied from 6 to 10. From 1869 to this day, the Court has always had 9 justices: 1 chief justice and 8 associate justices.

Every case that comes before the Court is given the name of the parties involved. If Mr. Jones is suing the US government, the case is called Jones v. the United States. When the justices decide a case, it becomes a **precedent**, which means that the decision becomes the basis for future rulings.

All Supreme Court justices are appointed by the president and approved by the Senate. They may hold their seats until they die. However, if a justice acts improperly or shows corruptness, the justice may be impeached and removed from the Court.

The Court's most important duty is to maintain the laws as they are presented in the US Constitution. The authors of the Constitution could not have known what life would be like in the 21st century. So, the Court interprets the Constitution for modern times.

The Court has many traditions. Since at least 1800, the justices have worn black robes at the Court, and white quill pens are placed on counsel tables each day that the Court is in session. This tradition dates back to the Court's earliest sessions. The justices also observe the tradition of the Conference handshake, which began in the late 1800s. As the justices assemble to go to the Bench, each justice shakes hands with the other 8 justices. This is to remind the justices that even though their opinions may differ, they are still united in support of a common purpose: to uphold the Constitution of the United States of America.

1. How has the Supreme Court changed over the years? Use evidence from the text to support your answer.

   _____

   _____

2. What does *precedent* mean?

   _____

3. When can a Supreme Court Justice be removed from the Court?

   _____

☀ Reflect

The author says the Supreme Court has many traditions. Why does the author call them traditions? How are they similar to what most people consider traditions?

_____

_____

Read. Then, answer the questions on page 36.

The Anasazi

One prehistoric civilization of the southwestern United States was the Anasazi. No one knows what the Anasazi called themselves. Anasazi is the name given to them by archaeologists and scholars who have studied prehistoric American Indians of the Southwest. *Anasazi* is a Navajo word that means "ancient enemy." Over time, the word has come to mean "ancient people." Some modern tribes prefer the term *Ancestral Puebloans* to the term *Anasazi*. However, *Anasazi* is the term that is most commonly used to describe the early people of the southwestern United States.

The Anasazi most likely came to the Southwest around 100 BC. They built simple homes with sticks and mud in shallow caves along canyon walls. They relied heavily on foods that they grew themselves, such as corn and squash. They were expert basket weavers, and therefore the first Anasazi phase is named the Early Basket Maker Period. This period lasted until around 500 AD.

The next Anasazi phase is the Modified Basket Maker Period. These Anasazi wanted to be closer to their crops, so they built their homes in open areas near the land they farmed. Their homes were called pit houses because they were built partially underground. During this period, the Anasazi still made baskets, but they also began making clay pots. Beans became an important crop because they could now be cooked over fires in clay pots. During this time, the Anasazi began wearing turquoise jewelry and using bows and arrows for hunting.

The Anasazi's third phase, the Developmental Pueblo Period, began around 700 AD. Their homes were above ground, but they built kivas, or ceremonial rooms, partially underground. They made pottery for two purposes: cooking and beauty.

The Great Pueblo Period began around 1050 AD. During this period, the Anasazi built cliff dwellings called pueblos, which looked like some of today's apartment buildings. They used ladders to get into the upper stories. They could pull these ladders inside to keep enemies from entering. Sometimes, several of these cliff dwellings were built near each other to form communities. These communities sometimes became the center for an entire region. Trade with nearby tribes began during this period.

It is not entirely clear what became of the Anasazi. Some people believe that the Anasazi were victims of a drought that caused them to abandon their pueblos and communities. Other people believe that fights with other tribes were responsible for the Anasazi's disappearance. By 1540 AD, only three of the Anasazi's major pueblo clusters remained occupied.

Name _____

Read the passage on page 35. Then, answer the questions.

1. Why is the first Anasazi phase named the Early Basket Maker Period? Use evidence from the text to support your answer.

_____

_____

_____

2. What is the main idea of paragraph 3? Write 2 supporting details.

Main Idea: _____

    Detail: _____

    Detail: _____

What is the main idea of paragraph 5? Write 2 supporting details.

Main Idea: _____

    Detail: _____

    Detail: _____

3. Describe the changes that occurred during the Anasazi's third phase. Use evidence from the text to support your answer.

_____

_____

_____

Reflect

How does the author describe how the Anasazi homes change over the three phases? How does this structure help your understanding of the passage?

_____

_____

_____

_____

_____

_____

_____

Name _____

Read the passage. Then, answer the questions.

Manatees

Manatees are gentle mammals that live their entire lives in the water. Their bodies are well suited to this environment. They have large, paddle-shaped tails and front flippers with toenails. Their skin is smooth with scattered bristly hairs. Manatees also have a thick layer of fat that keeps them warm in cool water.

Manatees are **herbivores**. They only eat plants, like water grasses. In warm weather, they search for food close to or in the ocean. In colder weather, they travel into warmer inland streams and lakes in search of food. Much like horses, manatees use their rubbery upper lips to gather grasses in their mouths, and then use their teeth to bite them off.

Manatees use touch and smell to communicate. They touch noses to give information. They also leave scent messages on stones or submerged logs. Manatees use scent glands located under their chins, forelegs, and tails.

Male and female manatees do not live together. They remain apart until it is time to mate. After mating, gestation lasts about 12 months. The mother manatee then cares for the infant for two years. She first feeds it milk, like other mammals, and later teaches it to eat sea grass. The young manatee rests on its mother's back while it sleeps.

Manatees are never aggressive. They will not fight, even to protect their young. In fact, they have no bodily weapons, like sharp teeth. They have no enemies except humans. Manatees are endangered only because people encroach on their habitats.

1. What are *herbivores*?

   _____

2. Describe how the manatee communicates. Use evidence from the text to support your answer.

   _____

3. In your own words, describe the interactions between a mother and infant manatee.

   _____

   _____

☀ Reflect

The author says manatees' bodies are well suited for their lives in the water. What evidence does the author give to support this point?

_____

_____

_____

Name _____

Read. Then, answer the questions on page 39.

Sleep Tight

Every living creature needs sleep. You may not realize it, but many important things happen to your body and mind while you sleep.

Getting enough sleep is extremely important. During sleep, your heart, lungs, muscles, nervous system, digestive system, and skeletal system rest and prepare for another day. Your body also repairs itself during sleep. Getting enough sleep helps your body fight sickness.

Insufficient sleep results in a sleep debt, or an amount of sleep that is owed to your body. Sleep debt affects how you function. People with this deficit may not think that they are sleepy, but they are less able to concentrate and learn new information. They may also be irritable and emotional, and their reaction times can be slower. In fact, some people with sleep debts can act in ways that mimic the symptoms of attention deficit disorder (ADD).

When you sleep, your body passes through a cycle that has five stages. In the first stage, you are either just beginning to fall asleep or are sleeping lightly. In the second stage of sleep, your breathing and heart rate become regular, and your body temperature starts to drop. The third and fourth stages are the deepest and most restful stages of sleep. In these stages, your muscles are relaxed, your breathing and heart rate are slow and regular, and energy is restored to your body. In the fifth and final stage of sleep, your brain gets the rest that it needs to function well the next day. During this stage of sleep, you reach and maintain REM (rapid eye movement), which means that your eyeballs move rapidly beneath your closed eyelids. REM is also the stage of sleep in which you dream. This entire sleep cycle takes about 90 minutes and is repeated five or six times every night.

Every individual has his own sleep needs, but researchers have determined the approximate amount of sleep needed by children. These times do not include time in bed spent reading, talking, or thinking about the next day. If you have trouble sleeping, there are some things that you can do to help you sleep better. The following list provides some suggestions for improving the quality of your sleep.

1. Establish a sleep schedule. Try to go to bed at the same time every night and wake up at the same time each morning.

2. Avoid foods and drinks that are caffeinated or high in sugar before bedtime.

3. Try not to eat large meals before bedtime.

4. Make sure that your bedroom is dark, cool, and quiet.

5. Exercise for at least 30 minutes each day, but not right before bedtime.

Name _____

Read the passage on page 38. Then, answer the questions.

1. What are the effects of insufficient sleep? Use evidence from the text to support your answer.

_____

_____

2. Based on the information in paragraph 4, summarize the five stages of sleep.

_____

_____

_____

3. What is the relationship between your health and sleep?

_____

_____

_____

4. Summarize the suggestions the author gives for improving quality of sleep.

_____

_____

_____

Reflect

In the first paragraph the author tells the reader that sleep is important. How does the author support this point throughout the passage?

_____

_____

_____

_____

_____

_____

Read. Then, answer the questions.

Maria Sklodowska

Maria Sklodowska, a famous chemist and physicist, was born on November 7, 1867, in what is now Warsaw, Poland. She grew up in the Russian area of Poland, where learning was considered a privilege. She was known for her amazing memory and learned to read at the age of four.

Sklodowska grew up without much money but was surrounded by science equipment. Her father was a professor of mathematics and physics. In 1891, she went to Paris, France, to become a student at the Sorbonne. There she signed her registration card with the French spelling of her first name, and her name became Marie.

Sklodowska received her physics degree in 1893, graduating first in her class, and her mathematics degree in 1894, graduating second in her class. She met the French physicist Pierre Curie, whom she later married, in 1895. The husband and wife team gained worldwide recognition for their scientific work. They studied uranium rays that penetrated like X-rays. Marie Curie named this occurrence radioactivity. The Curies discovered the elements radium and polonium. When they presented their findings in 1903, Marie Curie earned her doctorate. She is the only person ever to receive the Nobel Prize in both chemistry and physics. She later became the first female professor at the Sorbonne, and with the help of the French government and some friends and colleagues, she founded a radium institute. She died on July 4, 1934, of pernicious anemia. The condition was caused by her long exposure to radioactive materials.

1. What was Marie Curie's attitude towards learning? How do you know?

_____

_____

2. What is one conclusion you can draw about Marie Curie?

_____

_____

3. What were some of Marie Curie's accomplishments?

_____

_____

Reflect

How does the author organize the structure of the passage? How does this organization help readers understand the story?

_____

_____

Read. Then, answer the questions.

Louis Pasteur

Louis Pasteur, a famous chemist and bacteriologist, was born in 1822 in Dole, France. Pasteur was a doctor of science, but he was not a physician. Because he was not a medical doctor, many members of the medical profession did not take his work seriously. Pasteur, however, believed strongly that germs existed and that they caused disease. He eventually discovered a way to control the spread of a silkworm disease. He also developed vaccines for rabies and anthrax. It has been said that Louis Pasteur did more for medical progress than any other person of his time. One process that he developed is still used every day: pasteurization. This process keeps milk free from germs. It involves heating the milk to 140°F (60.00°C) for 30 minutes. The milk is then cooled quickly and sealed in sterile containers. Each time you drink a glass of cold, refreshing, germ-free milk, you have Louis Pasteur to thank.

In his later years, the importance of Pasteur's work was recognized by the medical community, and they invited him to speak at international medical meetings. In 1888, the Pasteur Institute, a research center, opened in Paris, France. Louis Pasteur directed the work that was done there until his death in 1895. Today, more than 100 years later, scientists at the institute continue to build on Pasteur's ideas.

1. How was Pasteur different from other medical doctors of his time?

_____

_____

2. How did Pasteur contribute to the medical field?

_____

_____

3. How did the medical community view Pasteur's work by the time he died?

_____

_____

☀ Reflect

How do Pasteur's achievements impact our lives today? Use evidence from the text to support your answer.

_____

_____

_____

_____

Read. Then, answer the questions.

Underwater Cities

Around the world, in warm and shallow waters, coral reefs are an underwater delight. A coral reef is like a complex city that supports a dazzling **array** of life. The surprising architects of these "cities" are little animals called coral polyps. Usually no bigger than peas, the coral polyps look like tiny flowers and are just as colorful.

The coral polyps extract calcium from the seawater around them. They convert the calcium into limestone and form little cups of rock to support their soft bodies. The coral polyps live in colonies with each polyp attached to its neighbor by the cup skeleton of its outer skin. As the polyps grow, they build new skeletons on top of the old ones. The limestone formations built by millions of coral polyps are called coral reefs. The structures formed by the polyps may be branches, cups, ripples, discs, fans, or columns. Each kind of coral grows in a specific pattern.

Coral reefs provide a habitat for many other animals. They are densely populated by an amazing diversity of marine life, including moray eels, sponges, tube worms, barracudas, sharks, starfish, manta rays, sea turtles, lobsters, crabs, shrimp, and fish.

Coral reefs are fragile, carefully balanced ecosystems that are easily threatened. A change in the temperature or quality of the water or a change in the amount of light that penetrates the water can kill the coral polyps. Some destruction of coral reefs results from natural causes, but humans cause the greatest damage to reefs. Once a reef is damaged, it may never recover. When that happens, the entire community is lost.

1. Summarize how coral reefs are formed.

_____

_____

2. How do coral reefs interact with their environment?

_____

_____

3. How are coral polyps threatened?

_____

_____

Reflect

Why does the author refer to coral reefs as "an underwater delight"? Use evidence from the text to support your answer.

_____

_____

Read the passages on pages 42 and 43. Then, answer the questions.

An Underwater Wilderness

The Great Barrier Reef is the largest coral reef system in the world. In fact, it's the only living system on Earth visible from space. Corals look like plants, but they are really animals. They have tube-shaped bodies with mouths on top. When corals die, their exoskeletons stay in place. Sand and small stones get washed between the skeletons. New coral grows on top of the old skeletons. The reef is built this way, layer by layer.

The Great Barrier Reef is not one reef. It is thousands of smaller reefs forming parts of a huge system. It is also made of hundreds of coral islands. The huge system stretches along the coast of Australia. It is more than 1,200 miles (1,931.21 km) long!

Between the reef and the beach is a lagoon. It is a great place for sea life because it is warm and quiet. Scuba divers love to dive there. There are more than 1,500 different kinds of fish living there, and more new species are discovered each year.

Divers also find many sizes of fish under the waves around the reef. Red dwarf gobies are less than one-half of an inch (1.27 cm) long. Whale sharks are the largest known living fish species and can grow to be more than 40 feet (12.19 m) long!

The reef is a great place for divers to explore because of the bright, colorful sea life. Divers might see one of the many shipwrecks. This part of the ocean is a hard place to sail because of its reefs, islands, and shallow water. Today, there are many lighthouses along the beaches to help ships steer clear of the dangers at the Great Barrier Reef.

1. How is the coral reef built?

_____

_____

2. Why is the lagoon a great place for sea life?

_____

_____

3. Why is the reef a great place for divers to explore?

_____

_____

Reflect

Compare and contrast "An Underwater Wilderness" and "Underwater Cities." What new information do you learn about coral reefs in "An Underwater Wilderness"?

_____

Read. Then, answer the questions.

Honey-Loving Stories

My name is Anna Hanks, and I come from honey-loving, beekeeping people. My grandpa, Hal Hanks, worked as a beekeeper in a small town in Idaho, a place that smells like sagebrush and has more cows than people.

Because my grandpa died when I was young, I never heard any beekeeping stories from him. So, I asked my mom to tell me her stories. They were sweet and fresh, like raw honey from a honeycomb.

Breathe Easily

"When I was young, I had asthma. I also had allergies to pollen, sagebrush, and the cottonwood trees by our house. It was so bad that at night, I could not lie down to sleep. One thing that helped me was chewing fresh beeswax with the warm honey still in it. That would open my nasal passages so that I could relax and breathe a little bit easier."

Baby-Soft Skin

"Each year, Dad sold the beeswax he gathered. He melted it into blocks and sold it to companies to be used in lipstick, lotion, candles, cosmetics, and soap. One of the benefits of beeswax and honey is that they soften everything they touch,especially skin.

Skinned Knees

"Every so often, someone would fall and skin a knee. Iodine stings, so nobody liked to put it on his scrape. Instead, we'd just put a dab of honey over the scrape and cover it with a clean bandage. Honey is an ancient **remedy** for cuts and scrapes. It kills bacteria and protects the scrape, and nobody ever said that the honey hurt!"

1. Based on the stories, what are the health benefits of honey?

_____

_____

2. What does *remedy* mean? How do you know?

_____

_____

☀ Reflect

How do you think the narrator feels about honey and beeswax? What does she say throughout the passage to make you think this?

_____

_____

_____

Read. Then, answer the questions.

Racket Sports

Tennis is played on a flat, rectangular area called a court. The sport is played on an outside court most of the time, but when the weather is cold or rainy, indoor courts may be available. A tennis court's size is different for singles (two players) and doubles (four players). The court's boundaries are marked with white lines on its floor. A net, which stretches across the middle of the court, divides it in half. There is a forecourt and a backcourt on each side of the net. Players on either side of the net hit the ball back and forth. Tennis is played with strung rackets and hollow rubber balls covered with fuzzy cloth. A tennis match is divided into either three or five sets. While only four points are needed to win each game, a player must win at least six games to win a set. When a player wins two of three or three of five sets, the player wins the match.

Squash is played indoors on a four-walled court. Red lines on the floor and walls of the court show the boundaries. A different-sized court and a different ball are used for singles and doubles. The singles' ball is soft and hollow. The doubles' ball is hard and hollow. Players use strung rackets to hit the ball against the four walls. In order to win, one side must have 15 points.

1. Write two main ideas from the passage. Write a detail to support each main idea.

_____

_____

_____

2. How is a singles tennis match different from a doubles tennis match?

_____

_____

3. How is singles squash different from doubles squash?

_____

_____

☀ Reflect

Compare and contrast tennis and squash. How are the sports related? Why do you think the author titled this passage "Racket Sports"?

_____

_____

_____

_____

Read. Then, answer the questions.

Infectious Disease

Viral infectious disease can be as frightening today as it was in the past when it meant probable death. Viral diseases are **contagious**. When they are not contained, they can become a health hazard. An epidemic is an infectious disease that affects a large number of people. The infection spreads outside of a limited group and lasts for a long time. The plague or "Black Death," spread through fleas infected by black rats, is one example of an epidemic. A pandemic is even more widespread than an epidemic. A pandemic is an infectious disease that is established across the world. Smallpox is an example of a pandemic. An endemic is an infectious disease present in certain areas or populations all of the time. It is often caused by an abnormality in plant or animal life exclusive to that area. Malaria, which is transported by the mosquito, is one example of an endemic. Through time, science has developed immunizations and medications to help fight some of these diseases and treat their symptoms. But for many, there is still no cure.

1. What does *contagious* mean? How do you know?

_____

_____

2. Describe the difference between an epidemic and a pandemic.

_____

_____

3. What causes an endemic? Use evidence from the text to support your answer.

_____

_____

Reflect

The passage begins by stating, "Viral infectious disease can be as frightening today as it was in the past when it meant probable death." How does the author support this point?

_____

_____

_____

_____

_____

Read. Then, answer the questions.

Shirley Temple: America's Little Princess

In the 1930s, Shirley Temple was the biggest little star in the world. Her movies helped people forget hard times during the Great Depression. She lifted spirits with her dimpled smile and trademark bouncy curls.

When she was born on April 23, 1928, in California, no one suspected what was in store for Shirley Jane Temple. It all started after a tap-dancing lesson. At the age of three, she was discovered by a young movie director. From there, she soon progressed to movie stardom. She made nine movies in 1934 and won a special Academy Award. Temple was the box-office champ for three straight years: 1936–1938. She beat out great adult stars like Clark Gable, Bing Crosby, Gary Cooper, and Joan Crawford.

Temple had a more normal life as a teenager. She went to an all-girls high school and enjoyed sodas, dances, and even schoolwork. As she grew older, her movies became less popular, and she gracefully retired from acting. Not long afterward, she met the love of her life, Charles Black, and married him in 1950. They had two children and were together almost 50 years.

Almost two decades later, Shirley Temple Black was back in the spotlight. She was running for the US Congress. She lost the election, but she went on to enjoy a long, successful career with the United Nations and the State Department. A battle with cancer only made the public admire her more. She survived and gave others hope.

One of her friends once said, "[Her mother's] wish was that Shirley would grow into a woman of character, faith, and usefulness, and she did."

1. How did Shirley Temple's life change from the time she was a little girl to her teenage years?

_____

_____

2. The passage states, "Shirley Temple was the biggest little star in the world." Underline the evidence the author provides to support this point.

3. What can you infer about Shirley Temple?

_____

_____

☀ Reflect

How does the author organize the passage? How does it help readers better understand Shirley Temple?

_____

_____

Name _____

Read. Then, answer the questions.

Fireflies

Fireflies are **bioluminescent** insects. This means they can produce their own light. They do this by mixing chemicals in their bodies. One chemical is common to all living things; it is called ATP. The other two chemicals are luciferin and luciferase. When all three are mixed with oxygen, the firefly is able to light its lantern, or the rear part of its body. The purpose of this light is to help find a mate. Each species of firefly has a specialized code. The code is made up of the number and length of flashes, the time between flashes, and the flight pattern while flashing. After mating, the female firefly lays about 100 eggs. Several days later, the female dies. When the eggs hatch, larvae emerge. The larvae are bioluminescent and sometimes called glowworms. The larvae eat during the spring, summer, and autumn months, sleep through two winters, and then progress into the next stage of their lives. They crawl into the soil, where they metamorphose, or change, into pupas. After about two months, they emerge as adult fireflies.

Firefly light is not hot. It is, however, very bright. Catching a few fireflies and putting them in a jar (with air holes) produces enough light to read in the dark. In some countries, fireflies are caught in nets and used as lanterns. People also use fireflies in festivals and wear them in small containers as jewelry.

1. What does it mean that fireflies are *bioluminescent* insects?

_____

2. What is the purpose of a firefly's light? How does it work?

_____

_____

3. Summarize what happens after the firefly egg hatches.

_____

_____

_____

Reflect

Why does the author include the last paragraph? What is the purpose of including this information?

_____

_____

_____

_____

© Carson-Dellosa · CD-104834 · Applying the Standards: Evidence-Based Reading

Read. Then, answer the questions.

Chambered Nautilus

The chambered nautilus is a modern living fossil. It is related to the cephalopods: octopuses, squids, and cuttlefish. Unlike its cousins, the nautilus has an external shell. The shell is made up of many chambers. The animal lives in the outermost chamber and uses the rest to regulate its buoyancy, or ability to sink and float. The chambered nautilus lives in the Indian and South Pacific Oceans. It finds its home at depths from 60 to 1,500 feet (18.28 m–457.20 m) along reef walls. On dark, moonless nights, it travels closer to the surface to eat tiny fishes, shrimp, and the molted shells of spiny lobsters. The chambered nautilus cannot change color or squirt ink like its relatives, but it does have arms. Two rows of 80 to 100 small tentacles surround its head. None have suckers to hold prey, but each can touch and taste. The nautilus lives longer than other cephalopods, sometimes up to 20 years. Unlike the octopus, it mates many times during its lifetime, each time attaching eggs to rocks, coral, or the seafloor. Each egg takes a year to hatch. Humans are the main threat to this ancient creature's continued survival. Well over 5,000 living nautiluses are harvested each year to supply shell dealers.

1. Where does a chambered nautilus find its prey?

_____

2. What are the nautilus's tentacles used for?

_____

3. How are humans a threat to the chambered nautilus?

_____

_____

✺ Reflect

Compare and contrast the chambered nautilus to other cephalopods. How does the author signal these similarities and differences in the text?

_____

_____

_____

_____

_____

Read. Then, answer the questions.

Stories of Immigration: The Truth about Angel Island

In 1882, Congress passed a law called the Chinese Exclusion Act. It was passed to keep Chinese people from coming to America. For years, Chinese workers had come to the United States to work as merchants or in mines. But some Americans were afraid that Chinese people would take their jobs and cause trouble. The 1882 law made it harder for Chinese people to enter the country. They were not allowed to be citizens until the Supreme Court said that anyone born in America was a citizen. This was important because families of citizens could **immigrate** to America.

At that time, there was a large section of San Francisco, California, called Chinatown. Thousands of Chinese people went there before the law was passed. In 1906, the San Francisco earthquake and the fire that it caused destroyed much of the city. When Chinatown burned, so did many citizenship records. The US government did not know which Chinese people coming to America were related to citizens.

In 1910, the government opened a station for immigrants on Angel Island in San Francisco Harbor. Each Chinese immigrant had to wait there until he could prove that he had a relative who was a citizen. People could spend months or even years there waiting to enter the United States. Some Chinese immigrants told their experiences through poetry that they carved on the walls of the wooden barracks where they lived.

The Chinese Exclusion Act was repealed in 1943. More than 250,000 Chinese immigrants came through Angel Island. Today, it is a state park with bike trails, hiking trails, camping spots, and boats. The barracks where immigrants lived are a historic site.

1. Why did Chinese people come to America? Why did some Americans not want them to come?

_____

_____

2. How did the earthquake and fire impact the Chinese people in Chinatown?

_____

_____

3. What does *immigrate* mean?

_____

☀ Reflect

Explain why "Stories of Immigration: The Truth about Angel Island" is a good title for this passage. Think of another title for this passage.

_____

_____

Read. Then, answer the questions on page 52.

Poems from Angel Island

Tour Guide: Welcome to the Angel Island Immigration Station. Surrounding you in these barracks are records of the people who stayed here from 1910 to 1940. What do you see on this wall?

Student 1: Writing has been carved into the wood, and it is in another language.

Tour Guide: The language is Chinese. Our translators, Lynn and Hai, will help us read what it says.

Lynn: This part says, "I took a raft and sailed the seas. Rising early at dawn with the stars above my head."

Hai: "Traveling deep into the night, the moon my companion."

Lynn: "Who knew my trip would be full of rain and snow?"

Tour Guide: Many Chinese people left their homes and sailed to America. When they got here, they had to wait to become citizens. They were detained in these small wooden barracks.

Student 2: Why did they write on the walls?

Tour Guide: Imagine you were forced to live in a place like this. How would you feel?

Student 3: I would feel angry or maybe sad.

Tour Guide: Other poems carved into the walls tell us more about how the Chinese people felt.

Lynn: Here, it says, "I have walked to the very edge of the earth. A dusty, windy journey. I am worn out. Who can save me? I am like a fish out of water."

Hai: "I worry for my parents, my wife, and my son. Do they have enough firewood and food?"

Lynn: "We are kept in a dark, filthy room. Who would have thought that my joy would turn into sorrow?"

Hai: "Cruel treatment, not one breath of air. Not much food, many restrictions. Here, even a proud man bows his head low."

Tour Guide: Thanks, Lynn and Hai, for translating today. We can learn from mistakes our country has made by studying history. That is why your teacher brought you here to the Angel Island Immigration Station. The words carved into this wall are preserved so that we can remember the past and learn from it.

Student 4: Thanks for showing us around. I will never forget it.

Read the passage and the play on pages 50 and 51. Then, answer the questions.

1. Based on the text, what were the experiences of the Chinese people at Angel Island?

   _____

   _____

   _____

2. What does "I am like a fish out of water" mean?

   _____

   _____

3. According to the play, why is it important to study history?

   _____

   _____

   _____

Reflect

Compare and contrast the passage and the play about Angel Island. How is the Chinese point of view presented in each text? What are the benefits of learning about this topic by reading the play?

_____

_____

_____

_____

_____

_____

_____

_____

_____

_____

_____

Name _____

Read. Then, answer the questions.

What a Wall!

The most famous wall in the world is not just one wall. Many people think that the Great Wall of China is one wall. It isn't. It's a series of walls and towers. There are open spaces between some sections. The wall is 3,000 miles (4,828.03 km) long.

Why was it built? The first wall was built in the third century to protect the border of China against enemies. In the 15th and 16th centuries, the wall of today was built for the same reason—to protect China. The tribes that lived north of the wall were **nomads**. They raided China for food and cloth. The wall helped keep them out. Guards stood on the towers and watched the border.

The Great Wall is the longest man-made structure on Earth. Millions of workers labored on the wall in the 1400s and 1500s. The emperor said to make it wide enough for six soldiers on horses to ride across its top. It took 200 years to finish.

The Great Wall snakes across hills but the wall is long and straight where it crosses plains and a desert. It ends at the Yellow Sea. The current wall was built using earth, stones, and bricks. Sections are made of materials that were found nearby. In the mountains, they often used stone. In the plains, builders used earth. And in the desert, they used sand.

Today, the Great Wall doesn't keep people out. In fact, it draws in many people. Some of the Great Wall has fallen or been destroyed over the years. Other parts are being fixed. Tourists from around the world visit the Great Wall, ruined or not. They can walk on its wide top and look across the hills and plains. It's like looking back in time.

1. Why was the Great Wall of China built?

_____

2. What are *nomads*?

_____

3. Write a summary of this passage.

_____

_____

_____

☀ Reflect

Explain why "What a Wall!" is a good title for this passage. Think of another title that could replace "What a Wall!" Use evidence from the text to support your answer.

_____

_____

Name _____

Read. Then, answer the questions.

From the Days of the Dinosaurs

The tuatara is special. It is just the same as it was 200 million years ago. It has not evolved. It used to live with dinosaurs. Now, it has a different roommate: a bird called a petrel.

Petrels are birds that make **burrows** in the sand. The tuatara moves in with the petrel. In some ways, this is a good deal. The petrel goes out during the day to look for food while the tuatara sleeps. The tuatara also watches the petrel chicks. But, if it gets hungry, it might have one of the chicks as a snack! It also eats insects and worms. Sometimes, it even eats a baby tuatara or two.

Tuataras look like two-foot-long (0.61 m) lizards, but they are not lizards. They are reptiles, but their closest relatives are all extinct. It has teeth that are part of its jawbone, and loose, soft green skin with scales. And, it has three eyes! It is born with a third eye that gets covered with scales as it grows up. Another amazing thing about a tuatara is how long it can hold its breath. It can go for one hour without breathing!

What about those babies? It takes them a long time to come into the world. Tuataras live to be 60 to 80 years old. They are not ready to mate until they are between 13 and 20 years old. Nine months after they mate, the female lays eggs. Then, it takes at least one year for the eggs to hatch! The parents do not raise the babies. Babies have to take care of themselves on the islands of New Zealand where this animal lives. Rats like to eat tuatara eggs, and wild dogs eat the babies. The tuatara is endangered. It's possible this strange leftover from the age of dinosaurs might soon be gone forever.

1. What does *burrows* mean?

_____

2. Describe the relationship between the tuatara and the petrel.

_____

_____

3. Based on the text, why do you think the tuatara is endangered?

_____

_____

☀ Reflect

The first sentence states that the tuatara is special. How does the author support this point throughout the passage?

_____

_____

Name _____

Read. Then, answer the questions on page 56.

The Great Lakes

The Great Lakes, located in North America, are the largest bodies of freshwater in the world. It is generally believed that they were made by glaciers that once covered the area. As the glaciers retreated, they gouged and filled the five Great Lakes as well as many other smaller lakes and rivers in the area.

Today, the Great Lakes are shared by two countries: the United States and Canada. The lakes provide people in the area with fresh water for drinking and for use in the home. They also assist many power plants and manufacturing companies. Recreation and transportation are two additional benefits. These lakes are also home to numerous freshwater fish like salmon, perch, trout, and walleye.

Lake Superior is the deepest of the five lakes. It also lies the farthest north. This lake is cold year-round and can develop violent storms. Because of this, many ships lie at the bottom of Lake Superior, including the famous *Edmund Fitzgerald*. The Soo Locks, completed in 1855, connect Lake Superior to Lake Huron, which is over 20 feet (6.09 m) lower. The locks were built to transport large ships and goods. Lake Superior is the largest freshwater lake in the world.

Lake Huron is named for an Indian tribe that once lived along its shores. This lake has more islands than any of the other four Great Lakes. Most of these islands are nearer to the Canadian border than the Michigan border. Lake Huron touches Lake Superior at the Soo Locks, Lake Michigan at the Straits of Mackinac, and Lake Erie to the south.

Lake Michigan is the only Great Lake located entirely within the United States. The rest share boundaries with Canada and the US Lake Michigan borders Wisconsin, Illinois, Indiana, and Michigan.

Lake Erie reaches the farthest south of any of the Great Lakes. It is also the shallowest. The most eastern Great Lake is Lake Ontario.

Read the passage on page 55. Then, answer the questions.

1. How were the Great Lakes formed?

_____

_____

2. How are the Great Lakes used by the people living on their borders?

_____

_____

3. Use the clues below and information in the text and map to complete the chart.

- The deepest Great Lake is also the largest.
- A lake that connects at the Straits of Mackinac has the second largest area.
- The shallowest lake is not the smallest in area.
- The lake without a Canadian border has the third largest area.

		Area (in square miles)				
		7,320	9,910	22,300	23,000	31,700
Great Lakes	Erie					
	Huron					
	Michigan					
	Ontario					
	Superior					

Lake Erie covers _____ square miles.

Lake Huron covers _____ square miles.

Lake Michigan covers _____ square miles.

Lake Ontario covers _____ square miles.

Lake Superior covers _____ square miles.

☀ Reflect

How does the map help you better understand the passage?

_____

_____

_____

_____

Read. Then, answer the questions.

The Unbroken Code

During World Wars I and II, hundreds of American Indians helped the United States military in a unique way. How did they do it? They became code talkers.

Because of safety, it was important for troops to send messages that no one could understand. American Indian tribes spoke their own languages and could send messages using these as codes. They could talk on radios about secret plans that no one could **decipher**. Enemy troops listened and tried to break the codes. But they couldn't.

During the wars, members of many tribes served as code talkers. The Navajos were one of the largest tribes with one of the hardest languages to learn. So, the biggest and most well-known group of code talkers was Navajo.

At first, there were 29 Navajo code talkers. They worked with the Marines to develop a code. Many words used in the military didn't exist in Navajo. The code talkers made a list of code words to match the military words. Airplanes were given bird names. For example, fighter planes were called "hummingbirds." Ships were given fish names. They also made codes for the letters of the alphabet. Any time they needed a word that didn't have a code, they would spell it using the alphabet code. After the 29 Navajo code talkers created the code, they left to serve in World War II. Then, new people were trained. By the end of the war, there were 400 Navajo code talkers. Their contribution was **invaluable**. Enemy listeners weren't able to understand their code. To this day, it's the only code used in a war that hasn't been broken.

1. Based on the text, why was it important to have codes during the wars?

_____

2. What does *decipher* mean?

_____

3. How did the Navajo code talkers work with the Marines in creating the military codes?

_____

_____

☀ Reflect

The end of the passage states that the contribution of the Navajo code talkers was *invaluable*. How does the author prove this throughout the text?

_____

_____

_____

Name _____

Read. Then, answer the questions.

Frank Lloyd Wright: American Architect

Frank Lloyd Wright was born in Wisconsin on June 8, 1867. He wanted to build buildings and had always been interested in architecture. He studied civil engineering at the University of Wisconsin. In 1887, he left school and moved to Chicago, Illinois, where he began his famous career. He became a designer for the firm of Adler and Sullivan, but by 1893, he left to establish his own business.

From the beginning, Wright used bold, original designs for his buildings. He rebelled against the more traditional designs favored by other architects. He believed that the design of a building should represent its purpose, its environment, and the type of materials that would be used in its construction. Wright created the idea of organic architecture, which means that a building should develop out of its natural surroundings. This concept is demonstrated in his famous Fallingwater house in Pennsylvania. The building was constructed on top of a waterfall and made use of sandstone cut from a nearby quarry, or a place where stone is **extracted**.

Throughout his years of work, Frank Lloyd Wright created many new construction techniques. Among them were indirect lighting, the use of steel-reinforced concrete blocks, and the inclusion of air-conditioning.

Architects who designed more traditional structures often criticized Wright's original ideas. However, Frank Lloyd Wright strongly influenced the development of modern architecture. Later in his life, he spent time writing, lecturing, and teaching. He established a workshop for apprentices who were studying his ideas and founded an organization to support their work. Frank Lloyd Wright died on April 9, 1959.

1. What are two character traits that describe Frank Lloyd Wright? Use evidence from the text to support your answer.

   _____

   _____

2. How does the author support the idea that Frank Wright contributed new construction techniques?

   _____

3. What does *extracted* mean?

   _____

☀ Reflect

Why do you think the author mentions the Fallingwater house in Pennsylvania? Use evidence from the text to support your answer.

_____

_____

Name _____

Read. Then, answer the questions.

A Ship without a Crew

   While out at sea in 1872, Captain Morehouse of the *Dei Gratia* saw a ship, the *Mary Celeste*. He knew the ship's captain, Benjamin Briggs. It appeared that something was wrong, but the *Mary Celeste* wasn't flying any flags to ask for help. Morehouse followed the ship and then sent his crew over. What they discovered terrified them.

   It was deserted! The cabin was wet, but the cargo was fine. Why did the people on the *Mary Celeste* leave?

   The crew towed the ship to land. A judge inspected it and discovered odd clues. A compass was smashed, tools needed to **navigate** the ship were missing, and the lifeboat and all of the papers had vanished. A broken rope was hanging over the back of the ship. Could it have been robbed? No. Money and cargo remained onboard. Could there have been a mutiny? There was no blood.

   This mystery has presented questions. There are theories regarding it. One person claimed to be a secret passenger. He said the captain dove into the sea to show that a man could swim fully clothed. The crew crowded onto a deck, which fell into the sea, and everyone was killed by sharks.

   Some people worried that the crew of the *Dei Gratia* had killed the people on the *Mary Celeste* to steal the cargo. Some wonder if the ship filled with water in a storm, so the captain told everyone to get into the lifeboat, and it sank.

   A ghost ship is scary because it reminds sailors of things that can go wrong. Maybe that's why the *Mary Celeste* has sailed from the sea into our imaginations.

1. What did the judge's inspection reveal?

_____

_____

2. What does *navigate* mean?

_____

3. Why did it seem unlikely that the ship was robbed?

_____

_____

☀ Reflect

The passage calls the story of the *Mary Celeste* a mystery. How does the author's writing make it feel mysterious?

_____

_____

Read. Then, answer the questions.

A Novel Approach

Taylor Caldwell was born in 1900. Her family lived in England. Her parents were very strict and made Taylor perform many chores. After her baby brother was born, Taylor also helped to care for him. When Taylor was only five years old, she won a national gold medal for an essay she had written at school. By the time she was six years old, Taylor was learning to read in French and Latin.

When Taylor was seven years old, she and her family **relocated** to the United States where she kept doing well at school. She won more awards for writing and also started to paint. She did much of the housework at home. At age 10, she found her first job working in a grocery store.

By the time Taylor was 15, she had a full-time job as a secretary. After her 10-hour work days, she went to high school at night. On the weekends, she cleaned her family's house, cooked, and did her homework. She almost never had a free minute.

Taylor was very busy, but she found the time to write stories. She started writing fiction when she was eight years old. By the time she was 12, she had written an entire novel. It was called *The Romance of Atlantis*. Nobody could believe it had been written by a 12-year-old!

Taylor went on to become a very famous writer. She wrote 30 novels. Many of them were best sellers. Late in her life, she said that all of the hard work during her childhood got her ready for a lifetime of writing books.

1. What does *relocated* mean?

_____

2. The passage states that Caldwell was busy. What evidence does the author give to support this point?

_____

_____

3. What is one character trait that describes Taylor Caldwell?

_____

☀ Reflect

How does the author organize the text structure of this passage? How does this organization help you understand the story?

_____

_____

_____

Name _____

Read. Then, answer the questions on page 62.

The Disappearing Island

Nauru (Na-ew-roo) is a tiny island about 26 miles (41.84 km) south of the equator. It is one of the world's smallest republics, and for the last 100 years, it has been shrinking slowly. Some might think that rising ocean levels are eroding the island, but people are to blame. Only about 10,000 people live on Nauru. However, most of them make a living by selling the island's soil. The soil contains rich minerals called phosphates. For nearly one hundred years, people have mined the phosphates to sell as fertilizer. The phosphates come from birds (or, more specifically, bird droppings).

Seabirds have nested on Nauru for thousands of years, and they covered the entire island with deep deposits of bird droppings. The native population did not seem to mind. The rich soil made it easy for them to grow food, and the sea provided all of the fish that they needed. It was a peaceful place, far from civilization. In 1798, the island was "discovered" by a British sea captain named John Fearn. He never set foot on the island, but he called it Pleasant Island because it looked like a tropical paradise covered with trees and flowers. The island was claimed by Germany in 1888. A few years later, a British company discovered the huge phosphate deposits and made a deal with the German government to start mining. In some places, the deposits were 50 feet (15.24 m) deep.

Australia took control of the island during World War I, but they lost it during World War II. After World War II, Australia, New Zealand, and Great Britain managed the island and mined phosphates. The country gained its independence in 1968 and took the name Nauru.

Even after independence, companies continued to strip away the soil and sell it. As a result, the Nauruan people are among the richest of any Pacific island. However, there is a problem. The coral island is only four miles (6.43 km) long and two miles (3.21 km) wide, and the supply of phosphates is quickly being depleted. The island is no longer a tropical paradise. Only a thin ring of soil surrounds a wasteland of barren rock. Nauru imports almost everything, including food and drinking water. Nauru exports nothing but phosphates. If the mining slows down, it could mean disaster for the economy. On the other hand, if people continue to mine phosphates, the island could disappear.

Australia, Great Britain, and New Zealand have agreed to pay $100 million for damages caused by the mining. This will temporarily help the people. Without a permanent solution, the island will keep disappearing under the Nauruans' feet.

Name _____

Read the passage on page 61. Then, answer the questions.

1. What did the native population appreciate about the island?

_____

_____

2. Why would it be a disaster for the island if mining slowed down? Use evidence from the text to support your answer.

_____

_____

_____

3. Give a detailed summary that explains how the birds have benefitted the island.

_____

_____

_____

_____

_____

Reflect

Based on the passage, who is to blame for the shrinking island? What evidence does the author give to support this point?

_____

_____

_____

_____

_____

_____

_____

_____

_____

Answer Key

Answers will vary but may include the answers provided. Accept all reasonable answers as long as students have proper evidence and support.

Page 5

1. personification; The wind makes the curtains move. 2. more sleep; He hasn't slept much and wants it to be night again. 3. sick; The narrator describes coughing, sneezing, a dripping nose, and a heated forehead.

Page 6

1. careful; She doesn't want the bird to fly away. 2. chronologically. Each stanza describes what the bird is doing in sequence. 3. A bird comes down the sidewalk and eats a worm. He then drinks dew from the grass, is offered a crumb from the narrator, and then flies away.

Page 8

1. She is determined and patient. 2. It felt like night was taking forever. 3. simile and personification ("bare feet"); to help the reader visualize her climbing the tree; 4. She discovered where the white heron hid its nest.

Page 9

1. On New Year's day, Jason spends time with his dog and eats a special breakfast with his family. He then takes down the holiday decorations and then watches the parade and football with his parents. They eat traditional foods and spend the day enjoying family time. 2. He is kind and helpful. 3. It's a day to relax and spend time with his family.

Page 10

1. 8 teams; 2. 8 games; 3. The only one. 4. She is athletic. She plays goalie and defense on a successful soccer team.

Page 11

1. sleep; 2. an owl's downy feathers; simile; 3. calm, quiet; *quiet moon, gently, soft snow*

Page 12

1. fingers pushing back a blanket; 2. shivering, standing, stretching, sparkle; They all start with *s*. 3. the night sky; 4. Both poems take place during winter. "Winter is a White Owl" compares winter to an owl. "Winter Sunrise" compares the winter sunrise to someone waking up. Both poems discuss snow. Both poems are one stanza.

Page 14

1. They are both athletic and enjoy swimming together. They swim some of the same events. Amy beats Mia in the backstroke event, and Mia beats Amy in the breaststroke event. 2. She is overwhelmed. 3. when her events would be and how long she would have for breaks and lunch; 4. indoor swimming pool

Page 15

1. It showed the individual snowflakes and made everything bright and sparkling. 2. She fell and lost the magnifying glass. 3. He enjoys playing with them. "Tug of war was his favorite game after 'knock down'."

Page 16

1. in a mocking way; 2. Jan is better at killing flies than Jeff is. Jeff has been careless letting the flies in and Jan is being responsible, trying to get rid of them before dinnertime. Jan has done research on how to kill flies and Jeff has not. 3. Last week she wasn't able to hit any flies.

Page 17

1. He wants to play but he has work to do. 2. Harry wants to focus on fun. Granny wants to focus on work. 3. different routes

Page 18

1. She likes him and wants to surprise him with dinner. 2. She asks her mom to pick up ingredients. 3. organized and thoughtful

Page 19

1. She was small and pushed around by other players. 2. She refused to give up, is a hard worker, and danced daily. 3. At the beginning she doesn't believe ballet is a real sport and doesn't want to try it, but by the end she loves it.

Page 20

1. brave; 2. sad, longing; *journeyed long, grew old, o'er his heart a shadow fell, strength failed him at length*; 3. No, the poem ends with the shadow telling him to look over the mountains and valley.

Page 21

1. It is important to find a balance in life. 2. The rocks, or most important things, won't fit. 3. He calls it "my jar" and says it was his choice to fill it this way.

Page 22

1. by describing how the animals call "good morning"; 2. continuing without interruption; 3. They both describe harsh and annoying sounds, which explain that Camper Two is unhappy.

Page 23

1. They were confused by the rhinoceros, a strange new animal. Check students' underlining. 2. The land, people, plants, and animals looked different. 3. unusual or strange

Page 25

1. Answers will vary. 2. Colter is helpful and brave. 3. strange, odd

Page 27

1. clever and determined; 2. The American Indians did not like him and wanted to kill him. Colter feared them. 3. in excess, a large amount

Page 29

1. She attended a stunt-flying exhibition. 2. She enjoyed being challenged. 3. She won awards and medals and became the first person to fly solo from Hawaii to Oakland.

Page 31

1. She loves and cherishes the tree. 2. She is a 13-year-old girl. The place is described from a child's perspective. 3. Its roots hold the sand in place. 4. Answers will vary.

Page 33

1. Answers will vary. 2. There are laws in place to protect the environment, and people "seem to genuinely care about the environment." 3. a slow, easy walk; stroll; 4. She enjoys learning new things. She is excited to share her new knowledge with her mom.

Page 34

1. Before 1869 there were 6 to 10 judges; now there are 9 judges. 2. a rule for future cases; 3. if they act improperly or show corruptness

Page 36

1. The people were expert basket weavers, and only made baskets. 2. Paragraph 3 describes the Modified Basket Maker period. Supporting details will vary. Paragraph 5 describes the Great Pueblo Period. Supporting details will vary. 3. They added ceremonial rooms called kivas, built partially underground, and made pottery for beauty as well as for cooking.

Page 37

1. plant-eating animals; 2. Through touching noses and leaving scents on stones and logs. 3. The mother takes care of the infant for two years by feeding it milk and teaching it to eat sea grass. The baby manatee sleeps on its mother's back.

Page 39

1. trouble concentrating, irritability, being emotional, slower reaction times; 2. In the first stage you are sleeping lightly. Then, in the second stage your breathing and heart rate change and the body temperature drops. In the third and fourth stages, your muscles relax and energy is restored. In the final stage your brain rests and you maintain rapid eye movement and dream. 3. During sleep your body systems get rest and your body repairs itself. Sleep also helps to fight off sickness. 4. Try to have a sleep schedule. Avoid caffeine, sugar, and large meals before bed. Exercise during the day. Make sure your room is comfortable, dark, and quiet.

Page 40

1. She was an avid, lifelong learner and saw learning as a privilege. 2. She was determined. 3. She was first in her class and the only person ever to receive a Nobel Prize in both chemistry and physics. She was the first female professor at Sorbonne.

Page 41

1. He believed that germs existed and caused disease. 2. He developed vaccines for rabies and anthrax as well as the process of pasteurization. 3. They took his work seriously and invited him to speak at international medical meetings.

Page 42

1. Coral reefs are formed as coral polyps get calcium from the seawater and convert it into limestone cups to support their bodies. They live in colonies and build new skeletons on top of the old ones to form coral reefs. 2. They provide a habitat for some animals. 3. by temperature, quality change in water, and human destruction

Page 43

1. Sand and small stones are added between coral skeletons, and new coral grows on the old skeletons layer by layer. 2. It is warm and quiet. 3. They can see bright, colorful sealife and shipwrecks.

Page 44

1. It can open nasal passages, soften skin, kill bacteria, and protect open wounds. 2. cure

Page 45

1. The passage focuses on tennis and squash. Supporting details will vary. 2. Only the court size is different. 3. The court size and type of ball change.

Page 46

1. spreading to other people; 2. An epidemic affects a large number of people and lasts a long time. A pandemic is more widespread and occurs across the world. 3. an abnormality in plant or animal life in a particular area

Page 47

1. As a little girl she was a big star, and as a teenager she had a normal life. 2. It lists the awards she has won despite great adult talent in the field. 3. She was a talented actress.

Page 48

1. They can produce their own light. 2. to help find a mate; There is a code that involves the number, length, and time of flashes. 3. The larvae come out and eat during the spring, summer, and autumn. They sleep through two winters and then they crawl into the soil to change into pupa. After two months, they emerge as adult fireflies.

Page 49

1. near the water's surface each night. 2. to touch and taste; 3. They harvest them to sell their shells.

Page 50

1. They came to work. Americans were afraid they would take their jobs and cause trouble. 2. It destroyed citizenship records that would prove immigrants' relationships to citizens and allow them into the country. 3. to come to a new country to live

Page 52

1. They were scared, tired, and living in dark, dirty places. 2. to be far from home in a strange environment; 3. To learn from the experiences of others and learn from mistakes of the past.

Page 53

1. to protect China against its enemies; 2. people who have no permanent home; 3. The Great Wall is the most famous wall in the world and is made of many walls and towers. It was built to protect China. Over time, some of the wall has been destroyed, and some parts have been fixed. Now the wall is a tourist attraction.

Page 54

1. digs a hole or tunnel; 2. They share the same habitat and the tuatara protects the petrel chicks. 3. It takes them a long time to mate, it takes a year for the eggs to hatch, and rats and wild dogs often eat the eggs and babies.

Page 56

1. Glaciers that once covered the area retreated, gouged out the land, and filled the holes as the ice melted. 2. People use the water in their homes and for drinking. The water also provides power, recreation, and a means of transportation. 3. Lake Erie, 9,910; Lake Huron, 23,000; Lake Michigan, 22,300; Lake Ontario, 7,320; Lake Superior, 31,700

Page 57

1. to communicate safely and protect secrets; 2. to solve or make meaning of; 3. Military terms were given code words, and there were codes for the alphabet.

Page 58

1. creative and determined; 2. The author lists the construction techniques Frank Lloyd Wright is responsible for, such as air conditioning, steel-reinforced concrete blocks, and indirect lighting. 3. pulled out or mined

Page 59

1. The cabin was wet; a compass was smashed; navigational tools, the lifeboat, and papers were missing; and a broken rope hung from the back of the ship. 2. to move or control; 3. There was money and cargo left onboard.

Page 60

1. moved to another place; 2. She worked a full-time job, went to school, and cooked, cleaned, and did homework on the weekends. 3. hard-working

Page 62

1. They could easily grow food, get fish, and live in peace. 2. It would decrease the money that comes into the country from its only export. 3. The birds covered the island with their droppings for thousands of years, which added valuable phosphates to the soil. The Nauru people have made money from selling the soil from the island, which is the only thing supporting Nauru's economy.